Practice Resurrection

STUDY GUIDE

Practice Resurrection

STUDY GUIDE

Eugene H. Peterson *&* Peter Santucci

WILLIAM B. EERDMANS PUBLISHING COMPANY
GRAND RAPIDS, MICHIGAN / CAMBRIDGE, U.K.

© 2010 William B. Eerdmans Publishing Company
All rights reserved

Published 2010 by
Wm. B. Eerdmans Publishing Co.
2140 Oak Industrial Drive N.E., Grand Rapids, Michigan 49505 /
P.O. Box 163, Cambridge CB3 9PU U.K.

Printed in the United States of America
www.eerdmans.com

20 19 18 17 16 15   7 6 5 4 3 2

Library of Congress Cataloging-in-Publication Data

Peterson, Eugene H.
Practice resurrection: study guide / Eugene H. Peterson & Peter Santucci.
p.   cm.
ISBN 978-0-8028-6552-6 (pbk.: alk. paper)
1. Bible. N.T. Ephesians — Textbooks.
I. Santucci, Peter.   II. Title.

BS2695.55.P48   2010
227'.5007 — dc22

2010006423

Practice Resurrection is published
in association with the literary agency of
Alive Communications, Inc.,
7680 Goddard Street, Suite 200, Colorado Springs, CO 80920
www.alivecommunications.com

Contents

CONTENTS

Contents

Preface

Every week, the congregation I serve meets to worship God. We don't do it perfectly, even after all these years, but we do it. There can be no doubt: We are a worshiping band of Jesus followers.

We spend a lot of time together, sharing meals and sharing lives, laughing and playing. We pay a lot of attention to the web of relationships that make up our community.

We spend a lot of time and energy and money in the good work of mission, serving the most vulnerable in our local community and sharing the good news of Jesus with as much imagination and care as we can.

Worship, community, and mission. We know that these are vital to the health of our congregation and we go about them with as much passion and creativity as we can muster. But growing up in Christ, growing into the fullness of life that Jesus said that he came to bring, this is where we enter murky waters. This is where most books fail. What does it look like to be mature in Christ?

Some people refer to "growing up in Christ" as discipleship. Others refer to it as spirituality. Here, Peterson introduces a new term: practice resurrection. But what exactly does that mean? How can you practice something that requires you to die first? How can you practice something you don't do yourself, but is done to you and for you by God alone?

We'll look at those questions a bit in the study guide for chapter 1. But suffice it to say, Peterson is after something completely different than what we're offered in most books on the Christian life. Practicing resurrection certainly can't be mastered like a technique. It can't be reduced to a formula. And it can't be figured out by taking a quiz in the back of some book.

Our American obsession with gathering information and mastering skills fails us when it comes to maturity in Christ. It has to. It is all about us and nothing about God. We use our information and skills as a replacement for God. Who needs God when you can do it all on your own?

Peterson's favorite word in this book is "comprehensive." You'll come across it again and again. And for good reason. What God is doing in Christ is comprehensive. Everything is covered. No detail is left out. In fact, things that you had never even considered before are included.

A few weeks ago, I was in a car accident. Fortunately, our EuroVan was covered by comprehensive insurance. So, when I talked with someone from the insurance company, she went through an amazingly long list of things that were covered by the policy. It was truly comprehensive. There was way more going on than I ever realized. I was literally covered.

The same is true with us in Christ. We are covered. Comprehensively. God is at work in ways we are mostly unaware of. Most of what's going on with us as we grow up in Christ has to do with what God has done and is doing.

Another of Peterson's favorite words is "participation." Resurrection is what God does, but practice is what we do. We are very much participants in this growing up in Christ. We get in on every bit of it.

But we don't get in on it alone. The God-created community of church is where it all comes together. And that's where this study guide comes in.

The problem with books is that they tend to be silent and solitary affairs. We head off to our favorite chair or sit on the bus and shut out the rest of the world. That's the worst way to get in on this practice of resurrection. If love is central to how we mature in Christ, sitting alone with a book isn't going to be much help. But if we engage in conversation with God's people, this worshiping community of Jesus followers that we love and struggle with, then we are well on our way to living what Peterson writes about.

In this guide, there is a summary of each chapter, followed by selected quotes from them. Sometimes a single quote is enough for a whole conversation. There are also questions drawn from every major point Peterson makes throughout each chapter. Finally, each section ends with a prayer drawn from the text of Ephesians covered in that chapter. Praying the text of Scripture is an ancient practice and since Ephesians is simply saturated with praying, it is easy to use its own language as prayer. In most cases, the text from Peterson's translation, *The Message,* has been slightly altered, simply changing the pronouns, to turn it into prayer. I suggest that leaders start a time of group prayer by reading/praying the Ephesians prayer in the study guide and then encouraging the rest of the group to pray in response to it.

Not only did Peterson's book arise out of four decades of small groups, classes, and conversations about Ephesians and the Christian life, but this study guide also comes out of many conversations. These conversations have included Peterson himself, fellow Regent College alumni, the worshiping community of First Presbyterian Church of Lebanon, and my children (Emett, Lydia Grace, Josiah, and Matthias) and always my wife, Charlene.

Epiphany 2010

PETER SANTUCCI

The Church of Ephesus (Eph. 1:1-2)

(pp. 1-29)

Summary

Birth is simple; growth is complex. Introducing people to Jesus, birthing new Christians, is fairly simple. But growing them up into mature Jesus followers? This harder task is woefully neglected. But Scripture is clear — God wants us to grow up. That's where Ephesians comes in. It is our primary text for maturing into a healthy, robust faith.

But before looking at Ephesians, we need to understand the term that gives Peterson's book its title: practice resurrection. Resurrection is not what we do; it's what God has done in Jesus. Jesus is powerfully alive and present with us as we go about this growing up in Christ. To practice resurrection, then, is to keep company with the resurrected Jesus as he leads us into maturity. This is essential: The same one who was in control of Jesus' resurrection is in control of our maturing. And that's not us. We don't get saved and then take over. From start to finish, it's God's work in us.

If practicing resurrection is the *what* of maturing in Christ, church is the *where*. Church is the context, but it's not an easy one and many drop out. It is easy to become disillusioned with church and to dismiss it as irrelevant and condescend to its unimpressive members. But church was not meant to be a utopian community, nor was it meant to be the answer to all the world's problems. Rather, Peterson states, "church as we have it provides the very conditions and proper company congenial for growing up in Christ, for becoming mature, for arriving at the measure of the stature of Christ" (p. 14). God intends the church to be as it is. On purpose.

Yes, on purpose. To help us get in on that purpose, Paul in Ephesians shows us what otherwise can't be seen: God's will, Christ's presence, the Spirit's work.

Ephesians is unique among the letters attributed to Paul. It's the one letter not written in response to a specific situation or set of problems. Instead of fixing something wrong, it sets out to establish something right. As such, it gives us not an image of a perfect church, but an image of what is actually going on under the hood of every messed-up but Jesus-following church. (It would be a mistake to read Ephesians in order to see what a perfect church would look like, because a perfect church has never existed. Ephesians isn't a how-to model for perfection, but a window into what the Trinity is doing in every church.)

If we see the church as a neglected structure, we'll try to renovate it. If the renovation doesn't meet our lofty romantic ideal, we'll move on and dismiss it. If we see the church as a business opportunity, we'll market it to targeted consumers to make them happy. But neither romantic images or pragmatic business strategies have an adequate imagination for church.

Church is a miracle, conceived by the Holy Spirit in the same miraculous way Jesus was conceived in his mother Mary. Just as surprising. Just as overlooked. Just as scandalous. Just as absurd. The elite and talented aren't the Holy Spirit's choice for forming congregations. The church, Peterson writes, "is the same Jesus story that is presently lived out in congregations . . ." (pp. 26-27). The same story. The same conditions.

We don't get to choose the members of our congregations. The Holy Spirit does. It's not obvious at first, but with a long, persistent, and loving look, the body of Christ can be seen in any congregation. Every outsider and even most insiders miss this. If we persist, as outsiders do, to try to see the church through romantic, crusader, or consumer lenses, we never like what we see. Rather, echoing Bonhoeffer's discussion of our wish-dreams of church in his book *Life Together*, Peterson writes, "The church we want becomes the enemy of the church we have" (p. 29). That is why we have Ephesians, correcting our view of church and restoring its place in God's work of growing us up in Christ.

Quotes to Consider

"Is it an exaggeration to say that birth has received far more attention in the American church than growth?" (p. 3)

"By delegating character formation, the life of prayer, the beauty of holiness — growing up in Christ — to specialized ministries or groups, we remove it from the center of the church's life." (p. 6)

"For far too long now, with full backing from our culture, we have let the vagaries of our emotional needs call the shots. For too long we have let ecclesiastical market analysts set the church's agenda." (p. 7)

"We live our lives in the practice of what we do not originate and cannot anticipate." (p. 8)

"Many Christians find church to be the most difficult aspect of being a Christian." (p. 11)

"Church is the core element in the strategy of the Holy Spirit for providing human witness and physical presence to the Jesus-inaugurated kingdom of God in this world." (p. 12)

"Church is the appointed gathering of named people in particular places who practice a life of resurrection in a world in which death gets the biggest headlines. . . ." (p. 12)

The practice of resurrection is an intentional, deliberate decision to believe and participate in resurrection *life*, life out of death, life that trumps death, life that is the last word, Jesus life." (p. 12)

"Church is not what we do; it is what God does, although we participate in it." (p. 17)

"None of us ever sees the church whole and complete. We have access only to something partial, sometimes distorted, always incomplete." (p. 17)

"Without Ephesians we would be left to guesswork, making up 'church' as we went along, and we'd be easy prey to every church fad that comes along." (p. 17)

"The first conception [by the Holy Spirit] gave us Jesus; the second conception gave us church." (p. 25)

"Paul's metaphor of the church as members of Christ's body is not a mere metaphor. Metaphors have teeth. They keep us grounded to what we see right before us." (p. 28)

"God does not work apart from sinful and flawed (forgiven, to be sure) men and women who are mostly without credentials." (p. 28)

3

"Romantic, crusader, and consumer representations of the church get in the way of recognizing the church for what it actually is." (p. 28)
"There are no 'successful' congregations in Scripture or in the history of the church." (p. 29)

Questions for Interaction

1. God wants us to grow up, to mature in Christ. Do you notice growth taking place in yourself over the years? How is such growth measured?

2. What does "practice resurrection" mean? How can we *practice* something only God can do?

3. Disillusionment with church is common. What things are you and others commonly disillusioned with about church?

4. Church is neither a utopian community nor the answer to all the world's problems, but a Holy Spirit-shaped context for growing us up. How does this change the way you think about church? How is the seemingly hodgepodge group of people the Spirit has placed you in essential to your practicing resurrection, growing up in Christ?

5. Many see the church as a neglected structure in need of renovation. Where do you see this attitude — yourself, others, books? In what ways might this be true? In what ways is it false?

6. Many see the church as a tool to target spiritual consumers. Where do you see this attitude at play? How does this twist the church's core identity and mission?

7. Peterson calls the church a miracle, conceived of the Holy Spirit, just as Jesus was — both unexpected, marginalized, and scandalous to outside observers. How is this direct continuity of the life, message, and mission of Jesus evident in the church? How is the rejection of Jesus by both secular and religious types evident in the church?

8. Why doesn't the Holy Spirit form congregations out of the elite? How would that miss the whole point of church?

9. What wish-dreams for the church do you have which make you an enemy of the church you deal with on an ongoing basis?

Praying from Ephesians 1:1-2

Lord, you have made us what we are, not by our own effort or will, but by your own will and the efforts of Jesus Christ. Saints! It's not a word we would have chosen for ourselves. It seems too grand, too holy, too perfect. But if that's what we are, what you're making of us, then give us eyes to see it, to see this holiness in us and in your people, both the ones we like and the ones we don't. In the company of your saints throughout time and right here in our own church, amen.

The Message to the Ephesians (Eph. 4:1, 7)

(pp. 30-49)

Summary

A set of balancing scales is the image behind the Greek word *axios*, which is translated as *worthy* in "live a life *worthy* of the calling to which you have been called" (Eph. 4:1). A balancing scale takes two different things — a lead weight and the item to be purchased — and matches them. They fit each other. God's calling and our lives are the two sides of the scale. Different but fitting. Peterson writes, "When our walking and God's calling are in balance, we are whole; we are living maturely, living responsively to God's calling, living congruent with the way God calls us into being" (p. 32). Chapters 1–3 of Ephesians deal with God's call and chapters 4–6 with our walking, our living in response.

We cannot weigh ourselves against ourselves; only in relation to God's calling.

God doesn't inform us. He calls us. The match to God's call is our personal, dynamic response. Abraham, Moses, the disciples, us — God calls and we respond. The Bible doesn't give us information about God to be discussed. It is God's word to us "to be listened to and obeyed, a word that gets us going. Fundamentally, it is a call: God calls us" (p. 34).

The scales aren't welded into place, but are dynamic, moving up and down according to the weight of our response to God's call.

This call and response is inherently personal, resolutely relational. And the more personal we become in our response to God in his call, the more personal we become with others. Rather than a simple one-on-one call and response, we enter into conversation with the community of those who are also personally responding to God. The primary place where this takes place isn't in small group meetings, but in regular worship gatherings.

Peterson uses Wallace Stevens's "Anecdote of the Jar" as a metaphor for worship. By simply being there, unexciting as it is, it reorients our world toward God. Things fall apart in our world and in our own lives, and we do all sorts of things to try to bring order to the mess. Worship brings order to our lives and world in ways that our efforts can't. But it does so as the jar does, from the center, not as a fence does, from the perimeter — centered order, not contained order.

In Ephesians, Paul pulls from Psalm 68, in which worship is an act of paying attention to God's word and action in the world which leads to human participation in that word and action. Worship as call and response. Paul also uses the psalm to point to the heavenly exchange, where Jesus ascends and give gifts as the Spirit descends, birthing the church. Jesus ascended is where we start when thinking of church and our lives of following him. Jesus ascended means Jesus is King. His rule extends not only over us, but over all. Worshiping Jesus the ascended King enables us to live a robust, wide-open life — the conditions necessary for practicing resurrection — instead of a timid, cautious life, intimidated by the powers around us. Though as King, he receives gifts from us, mostly he is the one doing the giving and we the receiving.

Everything we are and have is gift. We don't birth ourselves; we don't baptize ourselves. It's all gift, rising from the gift of the Spirit. As those who have received gifts, we become those who give gifts in community. As we grow up and into what we have been given, we become gifted givers. Peterson writes, "Implicit in each gift is an assignment. And we share the work with one another" (p. 47). Just as Jesus, in giving us gifts, invites us to work alongside him, we are inviting and being invited by the community formed by the Spirit to work alongside one another. As we do this together, there can be no rivalry or ownership, since it is all gift and none of what we do is done by our own power. We have work to do, but it is all gift-work. And as we do it, we grow up in Christ.

Quotes to Consider

"The Bible is not a book to carry around and read for information on God, but a voice to listen to." (p. 33)

"Call comes into our ears, beckoning us into the future, bringing us into a way of life that has never been experienced in just this way before: a promise, a new thing, a blessing, our place in the new creation, a resurrection life." (p. 34)

"We often start out looking for information *about* God, but we soon find ourselves developing the language of intimacy *with* God. . . ." (p. 34)

"Words, lively verbs and luminous nouns, severed from the living voice soon become dead leaves blown around by the wind." (p. 35)

"The life into which we grow to maturity in Christ is a life formed in community." (p. 35)

"Private worship while alone in semi-paralysis before a TV screen is not mature worship." (p. 36)

"What we must not do is deliberately exclude others from our worship or worship selectively with like-minded friends. . . . Maturity develops in worship as we develop in friendship with the friends of *God*, not just *our* preferred friends." (p. 36)

"One of the common dismissals of worship is that it is, well, so common. It is boring, nothing happens — 'I don't get anything out of it.' And so well-meaning people decide to put adrenaline in it." (p. 37)

"[Worship] isn't intended to make anything happen. Worship brings us into a presence in which God makes something happen." (p. 37)

"The order of worship works its way into the disorder almost imperceptibly as we sing and pray together, listen and obey and are blessed." (p. 38)

"Sanctuary is a set-apart place consecrated for worship, paying reverent attention to who God reveals himself to be and how he reveals himself in our history. The sanctuary is also a theater in which we find our place and our part for participating in the wide-ranging salvation drama." (p. 40)

"Maturity is not a patchwork affair assembled out of bits and pieces of disciplines and devotions, doctrines and causes. It is all the operations of the Trinity in the practice of resurrection." (p. 41)

"This kingdom life is a life of entering more and more into a world of gifts, and then, as we are able, using them in a working relationship with our Lord." (p. 46)

"We begin as gift. We don't make ourselves. We don't birth ourselves." (p. 46)

"If we are to become mature, we must gradually but surely realize ourselves as gift from first to last." (p. 46)

"Christ exercises his rule most conspicuously by giving gifts. The nature of Christ's sovereignty is not to lord it over his people, but to invite them into the exercise of his self-giving." (p. 49)

Questions for Interaction

1. We are to weigh our lives against God's call. What are other measures that people often weigh their lives against? What is the attraction of these other measures? What problems arise from them?

2. How does reading the Bible for information seem like obedience when it's really a means of distancing ourselves from the call of God to us in the scriptures?

3. If God's call is personal, why can't it be lived out apart from community? Why is conversation with the community of the called essential to living our calling?

4. Worship, like Stevens's jar, gives order to the world by giving it a new center. How does it do so? How is this redefining the center of the world as Jesus ultimately more effective and more important than bringing order by erecting fences (e.g., rules and other boundary markers)?

5. How does the ascension of Jesus to his rule over every power help us live a life worthy of our calling?

6. Though he's worthy to receive every gift from us, Jesus' rule is characterized by his giving of gifts to us. Why is it essential to live all of life as a gift? How does living and working as a gift take the air out of our self-importance and our rivalries?

7. Even the work Jesus gives us to do is a gift. Why is it important to do the work of ministry as a gift of participation in what God is doing as opposed to a job that our skills have earned us?

Praying from Ephesians 4:1

Lord, how can I live a life worthy of the calling you have called me to? How can any of us? Give me eyes to see what it is that you have done in Jesus, that I might live a life matched to it, a deeply relational life rooted in the church community. Reorient my whole world by a worshiping life. Everything I am and have is gift. Thank you! And thank you, too, for the active assignment implicit in each of these gifts. You are so good to let us partner with you in the work you are doing in the world. In Jesus. Amen.

God and His Glory (Eph. 1:3-14)

(pp. 53-68)

Summary

Sin has brought with it the spiritual disease of alienation. As Walker Percy puts it, we are "lost in the cosmos" — we don't know who or where we are; we don't know where we've come from or where we're going. We're lost. But God has done more than put up a few signposts. God is at work within the cosmos in Jesus and by the Spirit.

One symptom of our alienating lostness is debasing personal language into depersonalized facts, which turns people into functions and numbers. So, Paul launches Ephesians with one massive, exuberant 201-word sentence (Eph. 1:3-14). The staggering nature of this outburst gives witness to the vastness of what God has done and is right now doing in and around us. We need this in order to stretch our sin-shrunk imaginations.

We begin with God. As obvious as this might seem, we are not nearly as interested in God as we are in ourselves. In our self-preoccupation, Peterson writes, "Psychology trumps theology" (p. 56). We keep God safely in reserve on the sidelines while we do as we please with all the little stuff. Things seem to work out fine this way. But our souls atrophy. So, Paul restores our God-orientation with seven verbal rockets: *blessed, chose, destined, bestowed, lavished, made known,* and *gather up.* Each verb is an antidote to our lostness.

Blessed. God is actively pouring himself out for us.

Chose. We are not invisible or ignored. We are chosen. We're in on what God is doing.

Destined. Life isn't random. It's intentional. In God, we have a destiny. How we get to this destiny is beyond our understanding or control, so we simply receive it.

Bestowed. We are utterly drenched in grace, God's "delight in giving us what we could never imagine or guess" (p. 62). God isn't sitting still for a portrait. God is in action and the word we most often use to describe that action is "grace."

Lavished. God doesn't scrimp. "Lavish" is one of Paul's favorite words to describe the over-the-top abundance of God's gracing.

Made known. God doesn't keep us in the dark. He's let us in on what he's doing. What he's made known isn't something gossipy or top secret, but his purposes and methods. This isn't head knowledge, but knowing for wise living.

Gather up. We are connected to Christ like a body to its head. While abstraction is essential for science, it is deadly for relationship, and this gathering up all things under one head is personal and relational, not hierarchical or institutional. Coherence, not fragmentation. Unity, not dismemberment. This is what God is doing.

All these verbs have a destination: God's glory. Celebration. Praise.

But returning to his opening point, Peterson reminds us, "We are *in* the show. But we are not running it" (p. 68). With the inclusion and grace of these seven cascading verbs which save us from our lostness, it might be tempting to try to take over what we're now included in. But receptivity, not control, is the right response to grace. Receiving all this grace sets the context for maturing in Christ as we live to the praise of his glory.

Quotes to Consider

"If we calculate the nature of the world by what we can manage or explain, we end up living in a very small world." (p. 54)

"Sin shrinks our imaginations." (p. 54)

"Sometimes we have to change jobs in order to maintain our vocation." (p. 55)

"What God *does* comes out of who God *is*." (p. 57)

"There is no dividing God up into parts or attributes. God is who he is. We don't figure God out. We don't explain God. We don't define God. We worship God who is *as* he is." (p. 57)

"The moment we recognize that virtually everything that has to do with God takes place previous to our knowing anything about it, it becomes obvious that since we are not gods ourselves, we are forever unable to totally comprehend this 'everything.'" (p. 60)

"The God who destines/predestines cannot be depersonalized into a cosmic blueprint. . . ." (p. 61)

"We need to make ourselves conversant with the largeness, the sheer immensity of the world in which we are growing up in Christ." (p. 62)

"In matters of God's grace, hyperboles are understatements." (p. 63)

"We avoid the personal in order to avoid responsibility." (p. 66)

"We are relentless. We depersonalize God to an idea to be discussed. We reduce the people around us to resources to be used. We define ourselves as consumers to be satisfied." (p. 66)

"This is our destiny, this is what we are made for: a grand celebration in the full presence of God. Praise and glory." (p. 67)

"God starts everything. Everything. There is not a single verb [here] commanding us to do something, not so much as a hint or suggestion that we are to do anything at all." (p. 67)

"We are born into a cosmos in which all the requirements and conditions for growing up are not only in place but in action." (p. 68)

"The practice of resurrection is not a do-it-yourself self-help project. It is God's project, and he is engaged full-time in carrying it out." (p. 68)

"Anything we can come up with for ourselves in terms of goal or purpose is puny alongside of what is already in motion in the cosmos 'to the praise of his glory.'" (p. 68)

Questions for Interaction

1. In what ways is our culture obviously "lost in the cosmos"? In what ways do you experience this alienating lostness yourself?

2. It's common to leave God on the sidelines for big jobs while we take care of the rest. Why do we do this?

3. Do you have a sense of being chosen by God? How does being chosen change the way we live in a lost world?

4. Grace isn't just given; it is lavishly bestowed on us. Do you treat God as if he were stingy or lavish in grace? Where do you see grace at work right now?

5. Abstraction is the devil's tool, destroying what is personal. In what ways do you treat God more like an idea (an abstraction) and less like a Person? How does the abstract creep into and replace the personal in your relationships?

6. Why is it so hard to receive grace? Why do we keep trying to take over what God has graciously let us in on as participants?

7. God's glory is the end-game of all this grace. How much of your life is oriented toward your own glory? Toward God's glory? How does living in a world of God's grace reorient us toward God's glory?

Praying from Ephesians 1:3-14 *(The Message)*

Blessed God, what a blessing you are! Father of our Master, Jesus Christ, you take us to the high places of blessing in him. Long before you laid down the earth's foundations, you had us in mind, had settled on us as the focus of your love, to be made whole and holy by your love. Long, long ago you decided to adopt us into your family through Jesus Christ. (What pleasure you took in planning this!) You wanted us to enter into the celebration of your lavish gift-giving by the hand of your beloved Son.

Because of your sacrifice, Jesus Messiah, because of your blood poured out on the altar of the Cross, we're a free people — free of penalties and punishments chalked up by all our misdeeds. And not just barely free, either. Abundantly free! God, you thought of everything, provided for everything we could possibly need, letting us in on the plans you took such delight in making. You set it all out before us in Christ, a long-range plan in which everything would be brought together and summed up in him, everything in deepest heaven, everything on planet earth.

Jesus, it's in you that we find out who we are and what we are living for. Long before we first heard of you and got our hopes up, you had your eye on us, had designs on us for glorious living, part of the overall purpose you are working out in everything and everyone.

It's in you, Jesus, that we, once we heard the truth and believed it (this Message of our salvation), found ourselves home free — signed, sealed, and delivered by the Holy Spirit. This signet from you is the first installment on what's coming, a reminder that we'll get everything you have planned for us, a praising and glorious life. Amen.

Paul and the Saints (Eph. 1:15-23)

(pp. 69-87)

Summary

Prayer reorients us to the primacy of God's presence and action in our lives. It is the primary language we use in practicing resurrection, growing up in Christ. But prayer isn't just what we say. As Peterson puts it, "we need to have an existential understanding of prayer as an all-involving way of life" (p. 70). We are baptized. Our lives are immersed in God. Prayer provides a language suited for a life belonging to God. Most language doesn't take God or us or God in us seriously. Prayer does.

Paul soaks us in Ephesians prayer language. God blesses us. We pass the blessings on and they begin to accumulate. And as we continue to receive the blessing, it flowers into obedience.

Paul counts five gifts that God has blessed us with — wisdom and revelation, an enlightened heart, hope, the riches of his glorious inheritance, and the immeasurable greatness of his power. At first glance, they might seem a bit fluffy, but they've got power behind them. They are seen in Christ in God resurrecting him, seating him at his right hand, putting all things under his feet, and making him head over everything for the church. There is energy here that Peterson says "cannot be reduced to domesticated moralism or civilized good manners — or projected into a future that we will inhabit after death. This is the country that we live in. Here. Now" (p. 73).

Lists of kinds of praying can be useful at times, but they are ultimately limiting. Drawing from Martin Thornton, Peterson writes that prayer is "the act and acts that bring everything together in attention and offering to God" (p. 73). Not everything we say or do is prayer, but it all can be. We are, in fact, praying more than we are aware of praying. Models of prayer might be helpful in the beginning, but as we mature we grow into a thinking and living that is saturated with Jesus and Scripture, a praying that doesn't look like conventional praying but very much is prayer. Imitating formulas or other people in praying keeps us from experimenting, practicing, internalizing this God-initiated conversation. Prayer is an improvised living communion with God.

Not only are most of our conceptions about God wrong, but most of our conceptions about other people are wrong, too. We are in the company of saints. "Saint," not "Christian," is Paul's word for Jesus followers. It is the common word for all who are in Christ, not just the spiritual elite. We are defined not by what we can do for God, but by what God does in and for us. Our feelings about ourselves and others' treatment of us is of little consequence, how God feels about us and treats us is what determines reality. In fact, we can't truly be known apart from this word. We *are* saints. This forces us to see ourselves and others differently. "Saint" gives us a word that speaks the truth about who we really are — God's people — in a world that steadfastly ignores this primary reality about us. We are immersed, plunged into a God-defined reality. No more settling for numbers or functions or genealogies to determine who we are.

Saints aren't necessarily pious. Piety comes from us. Holiness comes from God. It's what he does to us and in us. We are just as bad and messy as everyone else — God knows who he's dealing with — but we are saints, we are those baptized into the operations of the Trinity. The sports teams we support, our sexual practices, our jobs, our IQ — these are all important, but none of them defines us, none of them gives us a true identity. Baptism defines us, gives us an identity.

Like Mt. Monadnock, the resurrection life is easy to be right on top of and never see. We get so preoccupied we may never see it. But that doesn't mean it's not there. It's all right there under our feet.

Quotes to Consider

"God is actively at work among us for our good and our salvation; he is not passive. God is present and personal; he is not remote. God is totally involved in the cosmos; he is not indifferent." (p. 69)

"We start with God. If we start with ourselves, we wander farther into the dark woods." (p. 70)

"[Prayer] is a way of using language personally in response to and in the presence of God, and in response to and in the company of the saints." (p. 70)

"Baptism redefines our life as God's gift to be lived in the presence and within the operations of God." (p. 70)

"Most of our social experience with language takes place with people who could not care less about our true God-given identity and who have little interest in resurrection." (p. 71)

"We participate in everything that Christ does." (p. 73)

Martin Thornton: "Prayer, quite simply, is the total experience of the Christian man and woman." (p. 74)

"He [Paul] names us saints — not because we are so wonderful but because he sees us truly as ever and always in the company of the Holy Trinity: holy men, holy women, holy children, holy, holy, holy." (p. 79)

"The most important thing about any one of us is not what we do for God, but what God does for us." (p. 80)

"Our identity is not something exterior to us, a label, a name tag. We live out our identity in the practice of resurrection." (p. 83)

"Everything revealed in our Scriptures can be lived by flesh-and-blood men and women like us." (p. 83)

"God reveals himself in personal relationship and only in personal relationship. God is not a phenomenon to be considered. God is not a force to be used. God is not a proposition to be argued. There is nothing in or of God that is impersonal, nothing abstract, nothing imposed." (p. 87)

Questions for Interaction

1. People often live fearfully, assuming God is passive, distant, or indifferent. Why do we often live this way? How would knowing God's active, personal presence in the world help you to be less fearful and not so in need for control?

2. God does his maturing work in us in community. Why in community? Why not let us work it out on our own on long walks in the woods or in desert caves?

3. How has using formulas or examples of prayer been helpful for you? How do such patterns limit and stunt your growth in prayer?

4. We pray more often than we realize, because all of life *can* (but isn't necessarily) prayer. How is this so? How can more of our living become praying?

5. Every Jesus-follower is a saint, not just the special ones. How does this change your perception of yourself? How does this change your perception of the often frustrating people around you?

6. We create identities for ourselves out of all sorts of feelings and practices, but baptism into the Trinity is to be our one and only identity. What other things or practices have you used to identify yourself? What would it be like to let them go and only identify yourself in Christ? How would this refusal to identify anyone outside of God change your relationships?

7. Like Mt. Monadnock, just because you can't "see" holiness in yourself and others doesn't mean it's not there. How does the Mt. Monadnock story help you understand better the way that God goes about working holiness in us? What frustrates you about this approach?

Praying from Ephesians 1:17-21 (TNIV)

Glorious Father, God of our Lord Jesus Christ, give us the Spirit of wisdom and revelation, so that we may know you better. May the eyes of our hearts be enlightened in order that we may know the hope to which you have called us, the riches of your glorious inheritance in your people, and your incomparably great power for us who believe — the same power as the mighty strength you exerted when you raised Christ from the dead and seated him at your right hand in the heavenly realms, far above all rule and authority, power and dominion, and every name that can be invoked, not only in the present age but also in the one to come. Amen.

Grace and Good Works (Eph. 2:1-10)

(pp. 88-106)

Summary

The reality is about practicing resurrection. We were dead in sin. But we are now alive in Jesus through resurrection. We no longer live in death country, we live in resurrection country.

In our self-made, competitive culture, we need to acquire passivity.

We have advanced in almost every outward way in our culture, but we haven't matured. We've chosen technology and success over the soul. Our Hebrew ancestors were energetically countercultural on this matter. And our Christian ancestors were insistent on Jesus crucified, the cross being a universal symbol of rejection, humiliation, and failure. Peterson calls any attempt to blend with culture on this matter an antichrist.

An acquired passivity is essential to grace. Grace is received or it is nothing. Like water to a swimmer, grace isn't an action we do; it's what we participate in. Faith is diving into this sea of grace. The problem is that we like our feet firmly on the ground, with us firmly in control. The hardest thing for us, Peterson writes, is this "reorientation from living anxiously by my wits and muscle to living effortlessly in the world of God's active presence" (p. 96).

Work is good and we continue to do it — unemployment or underemployment aren't spiritual virtues. God works. From creation on, God has been at work and is right now at work. He invites us to join him in his work, right here in his workplace.

God's work comes to us as grace, as sheer gift. Creation: gift. Salvation: gift. It's all free. No necessity. No demand. God's work and our work within his work all point to grace.

Grace is unseen. But it becomes seen when we work, taking what has been given to us and shaping that grace into something that can be seen. Likewise, God is invisible. But God's glory becomes seen when Jesus works. Our participation in that work also gives visible form to God's glory. The good works God has created us for are no less tangible and physical than we are.

There are two distortions of work.

The secularist romanticizes work, turning it into a method for gaining significance. As we watch the payoffs roll in, we gain job satisfaction. We become godlike without God. We skip our work-restraining Sabbaths in an act of self-worship, self-idolatry.

The pietist spiritualizes work into religious activity — prayer, worship, witness — in a way that dismisses everyday work as secondary at best. But Jesus' metaphors for the kingdom of God and his own work itself were located solidly in secular work settings.

Almost any work setting can also be a container for grace and the setting for our practice of resurrection.

Quotes to Consider

"When the wild bull of American ambition is bred with a tame Christianity with no cross, the result is mongrel spirituality — a 'Christian' with both the image of God and the crucified Savior lost in the cross-breeding. . . . An antichrist?" (p. 93)

"The air we breathe and the atmosphere we inhabit as believers and followers of Jesus is grace." (p. 93)

"Grace is an insubstantial, invisible reality that permeates all that we are, think, speak, and do." (p. 94)

"Faith in Christ is an act of abandoning the shores of self, where we think we know where we stand and where if we just try hard enough we can be in control. Faith in Christ is a plunge into grace." (p. 95)

"Fundamentally, work is not what we do; we are the work that God does." (pp. 98-99)

"Grace does not displace work. . . . Work is not downgraded to something sub-spiritual." (p. 99)

"All our work is preceded by his work. All our work takes place in God's workplace." (p. 99)

"All work at its heart and origin gives form to a gift. Or, to put it another way, it is the nature of work to provide a container for a gift." (p. 101)

"Nothing in the Christian life matures apart from work and works." (p. 101)

"God's glory is God's invisibility become visible in Jesus at work." (p. 102)

"God's grace, the basic giftedness of everything that God is and does, becomes present to us exclusively in the form of work." (p. 102)

"The visible creation is the form, the context, in which we experience grace." (p. 103)

"Good work and good works are to grace what a pail is to water: a container to get it from the well to the supper table. God's grace is the content. Our work (after the manner of Jesus) is the container." (p. 103)

"Nothing in the practice of resurrection is experienced or participated in apart from a body." (p. 103)

"Work is the generic form for embodying grace." (p. 103)

Questions for Interaction

1. Grace is difficult for self-made people to receive. How easy or difficult is it for you to receive grace? How do your past and present successes and failures contribute to your ability and inability to receive grace?

2. How does our culture's emphasis on technology and success do damage to the soul?

3. What does Peterson mean by an "acquired passivity"? And why is it essential for receiving grace?

4. How does an understanding of God-as-worker shape our appreciation for work?

5. How does the secular romanticizing of work lead to self-idolatry?

6. How does the religious spiritualizing of work lead to the dismissal of everyday work and God's use of it in the world?

7. How can the same job be either a participation in grace or a distortion (either romantic or spiritualized) of the good work God has given us to do?

Praying from Ephesians 2:1-10 *(The Message)*

God, it wasn't so long ago that we were mired in that old stagnant life of sin. We let the world, which doesn't know the first thing about living, tell us how to live. We filled our lungs with polluted unbelief, and then exhaled disobedience. We all did it, all of us doing what we felt like doing, when we felt like doing it, all of us in the same boat. It's a wonder, God, that you didn't lose your temper and do away with the whole lot of us. Instead, immense in mercy and with an incredible love, you embraced us. You took our sin-dead lives and made us alive in Christ. You did all this on your own, with no help from us! Then you picked us up and set us down in highest heaven in company with Jesus, our Messiah.

Now you have us where you want us, with all the time in this world and the next to shower grace and kindness upon us in Christ Jesus. Saving is all your idea, and all your work. Help us trust you enough to let you do it. It's your gift from start to finish! We don't play the major role. If we did, we'd probably go around bragging that we'd done the whole thing! No, we neither make nor save ourselves. You do both the making and saving. You create each of us by Christ Jesus to join you in the work you do, the good work you got ready for us to do, work we had better be doing.

Peace and the Broken Wall (Eph. 2:11-22)

(pp. 109-128)

Summary

If practicing resurrection is about growing up in Christ, individualism is one of its greatest enemies. It tries to serve God without dealing with God, to love neighbors without getting to know their names. Church is its antidote, a relational immersion where both God and people are taken seriously and dealt with in real, non-abstract ways.

Church cannot be measured, experienced, or understood from the outside. What you see is not what you get. Therefore, most commentary on church and programs for fixing the church are useless. Too often, Americans think functionally about the church — what it is doing and what it really ought to be doing. We need to be thinking ontologically about the church — what it *is*.

What we can't actually see in church is God. Church is the body of Jesus, the residence of the Spirit. We are included in what is going on, but only passively so. Church is the work of God. Peterson writes, "We have to submit ourselves to the revelation and receive church as the gift of Christ as he embodies himself in the world" (p. 118).

Just as Jesus has a dual nature — fully human and fully divine — so, too, does the church. It is fully human in the people who make it up, and it is fully divine in the presence of the Spirit. It is the body of Christ.

Any attempt to create the church on our own, including who we want and excluding those we don't (our "Gentiles"), denies what the church is: God's creation. "We do not create the church," Peterson writes.

"It *is*. We enter and participate in what is given to us" (p. 121). Yes, there is plenty that we do. Lots. But most of church is what God does, not us.

At the same time as we have those who are trying to create (or re-create) the church, trying way too hard, we have those who sit in the bleachers and don't participate. Both miss out on the depth of what is actually going on. A third group simply gives up and looks for something else more suited to them. Peterson writes, "If we don't grasp church as Christ's body, we will always be dissatisfied, impatient, angry, dismayed, or disgusted with what we see" (p. 124).

Jesus is our peace — bringing us home, bringing us together, breaking down hostility, re-creating us as a unified humanity, and reconciling us to God. If that's so, why isn't church the most peaceful place on earth?

First, peace is personal, not an idea, and requires participation. Second, Jesus forces nothing on us, leaving us to choose to participate or not. Third, peace requires sacrifice, the cross. In all the world, these three only come together in the church. But because we are all in process of becoming mature, Christ's peace is always in process among us. Christ is always making peace while he is making us.

Quotes to Consider

"God accounts for most of what is going on in the world." (p. 110)

"We need to know that in and with, before and after everything that is and takes place, God is present and active." (p. 110)

"We need to know that God is not just 'deity in general,' not off doing something big in the universe, remote from who we are or what we think of ourselves. God is not remote; God is present and active in us." (p. 111)

"God has to do with every part of our lives, not just the religious part." (p. 111)

"Individualism is the growth-stunting, maturity-inhibiting habit of understanding growth as an isolated self-project. Individualism is self-ism with a swagger." (p. 112)

"If grace and good works are separated, either one by itself becomes a breeding ground for individualism: living a 'spiritual' life (or intellectual or caring or devout) without it taking bodily form; living a 'practical' life (working for God, helping humanity, leading good causes) without personal relationship. Briefly, specializing in God (grace) without being bothered with people; specializing in people (good works) without bothering with God." (p. 113)

"Church summarizes all that God does, all that Christ is, all that we are in Christ. Church comprises all that is involved in living the mature life in Christ." (p. 113)

"The huge reality of God already at work in all the operations of the Trinity is benched on the sideline while we call timeout, huddle together with our heads bowed, and figure out a strategy by which we can compensate for God's regrettable retreat into invisibility." (p. 118)

"Church is not something that we cobble together to do something for God. It is the 'fullness of him who fills all in all' (Eph. 1:23) working comprehensively with and for us." (p. 119)

"Remember this well, for church cannot be comprehended by negatives, by what it is not." (p. 120)

"Most of what the church is, not all, is invisible. We miss the complexity and glory of church if we insist on measuring and defining it by the parts we play in it, if we insist on evaluating and judging it by what we think it *ought* to be." (p. 121)

"Peace cannot be achieved in impersonal ways. It is not a strategy, not a program, not a political action, not an educational process." (p. 125)

"Peace is always in process, never a finished product." (p. 125)

"Church is the place where God cannot be depersonalized into an idea or force." (p. 125)

"[W]hen anyone looks at church as a performance, whether from inside or outside, mostly what they see is skinned knees and sprained ankles, awkward, bungled attempts at keeping the peace. But we also know that at the source and center of the church, Jesus is our peace. And so we don't quit." (p. 127)

"When we consider church, we must not be more spiritual than God." (p. 128)

Questions for Interaction

1. Individualism is the hallmark of American identity. Why is it so detrimental to growing up in Christ? How is church God's solution to the problem of our individualism?

2. Church cannot be measured or understood from the outside. How much evaluation of your church do you do using external measures? Why do we so easily miss out on all that God is doing in the center of the church?

3. What attempts have you made to "fix" the church? How successful have they been? Why is that theologically inappropriate?

4. When have you been dissatisfied, impatient, angry, dismayed, or disgusted with church? What were you seeing to feel that way? What were you missing out on to feel that way?

5. Jesus is our peace. How has God used the church to bring peace to your life?

6. Why isn't the church a place of continual peaceful bliss?

7. What would help you to keep seeing church as a gift from God?

Praying from Ephesians 2:11-22 *(The Message)*

Lord, it seems like only yesterday that we were outsiders to your ways, not knowing the first thing about the way you work, without the faintest idea of Christ. But now, because of Christ — dying that death, shedding that blood — we are in on everything.

You tore down the wall we used to keep each other at a distance. You got rid of everything in the way and started over. You created a new kind of human being, a fresh start for everybody. Jesus, you brought us together through your death on the cross. The cross got us to embrace, and that was the end of the hostility. You came and preached peace to outsiders and insiders. You treated us as equals, and so made us equals. Through you we all share the same Spirit and have equal access to the Father.

Because of you, we're no longer wandering exiles. This kingdom of faith is now our home country. We're no longer strangers or outsiders. And you, God, are building a home. You're using us all — irrespective of how we got here — in what you're building. You used the apostles and prophets for the foundation. Now you're using us, fitting us in brick by brick, stone by stone, with Christ Jesus as the cornerstone that holds all the parts together. We see it taking shape day after day — a holy temple built by you, all of us built into it, a temple in which you are quite at home.

Help us to live this reality. Amen.

Church and God's Manifold Wisdom (Eph. 3:1-13)

(pp. 129-146)

Summary

Jesus is the head of the church and we are his body. The two only work together and cannot be understood apart from each other. Jesus and church can only be understood in relation to one another. And as long as we think about and act as if church is an add-on to our lives which have Me at the center, we miss out on it and on Jesus.

Since the mature resurrection life is personal, not abstract, Paul shares some of his story in Ephesians. But he does so cautiously, giving witness, not drawing attention. And because it's personal, it never passes over real people in pursuit of its goal.

But people don't want neighbors. Impatient with relationships, we prefer self-sufficient independence. This cultural context surrounding us seeps into the church, requiring us to re-imagine just what church is. Growing up is going to require some growing pains.

Any attempt to analyze the church by the names, dates, and locations of history is worthless. While the church exists in history, it is not a function of history. It is, as Peterson puts it, the "life of Christ, the work of the Spirit, the plan of God" (p. 137) incarnated in human community. Peterson writes, "Church is the workshop for turning knowledge into wisdom, becoming what we know" (p. 138).

The poet Gerard Manley Hopkins coined the word "inscape." Whereas landscape refers to what is exterior and describable, inscape is what is interior and unique to a person. Artists make us aware of inscape,

29

revealing the unique internal qualities of people and things we carelessly pass by. It is so easy to miss the inscape of church, judging the church by external qualities — a bunch of old people, a mediocre choir, a rocking praise band, a highly coordinated small group program, whatever — and miss out on the texture of grace that is the real artwork of the Spirit in the lives of this unique people. Where people reduce church to buildings, demographics, and historical embarrassments, we refuse to let those obvious externals keep us from seeing the deep Trinity-shaped inscape. Seeing a church's inscape keeps us from getting stuck in passing irritants or caught up in passing fads.

The church has a facade of ordinariness. But if we stop looking at ourselves for a moment, we'll see the shadow work of the glorious Trinity going on.

Quotes to Consider

"The Christian life is too often treated in our culture as an extra, something we get involved in after we have the basic survival needs established and then realize that things aren't yet quite complete." (p. 130)

"Christ is *always* present, for *all* of us. Just because we have no awareness of the presence and action of God previous to our knowledge of it does not mean that God was absent." (p. 130)

"Church is not an 'add-on,' a program or cheerleader, to help us be faithful and better Christians." (p. 131)

"This resurrection life is never disembodied, never abstract, never an objective truth that can be analyzed and argued and defended." (p. 132)

"The mature life in Christ does not dillydally. It doesn't chase after fads. But any focus on a goal that dismisses, ignores, and avoids spouse, children, and neighbors who are perceived as impediments to pressing on to the 'heavenly call' simple doesn't understand the way the *goal* functions in a mature life." (p. 133)

"Maturity cannot be hurried, programmed, or tinkered with. There are no steroids available for growing up in Christ more quickly. Impatient shortcuts land us in the dead ends of immaturity." (p. 133)

"Church cannot be objectively described or defined from the outside. Church can only be entered." (p. 137)

"Artists make us insiders to the complexity and beauty of what we deal
with everyday but so often miss." (p. 139)

"The artist helps us see what we have always seen but never seen." (p. 139)

"Church as the body of Christ is not obvious. But neither is Jesus as the
savior of the world obvious." (p. 145)

"As long as we think that the church is in competition with the world, a
way of outdoing the world, we will never get it." (p. 146)

"American culture is doing its dead level best with its celebrities, consumerism, and violence to keep us in a perpetually arrested state of adolescence." (p. 146)

Questions for Interaction

1. It is easy to think of "Christian" as an add-on to our lives, and
   "church" as an add-on to our Christian lives. What things do we do
   or say that betray this add-on view of life? What does this me-in-
   the-center approach do to our maturity in Christ?

2. When have you recently passed over real people in pursuit of an abstract goal?

3. Landscape deals with exterior, describable qualities; inscape with
   interior, unique qualities. What is the landscape of your church?
   What is its inscape?

4. How often do we deal with church purely on landscape, completely
   passing over its inscape? What's the problem with this way too
   common practice of ignoring a church's inscape?

5. Who can help you keep your church's inscape in front of your praying imagination?

Praying from Ephesians 3:1-13 *(The Message)*

Lord, open our eyes to see into the mystery of Christ — the
mystery that people who have never heard of you and those
who have heard of you all their lives stand on the same
ground before you. We get the same offer, same help, same
promises in Christ Jesus. The Message is accessible and welcoming to every one of us, across the board.

Help us to understand and respond to this Message, which comes to us as sheer gift, with you handling all the details.

And so here we are, in way over our heads, swimming in your inexhaustible riches and generosity. Help us to get others in on it, too. Use Jesus-followers gathered in churches like ours to make known this extraordinary plan of God.

In you, we're free to say whatever needs to be said, bold to go wherever we need to go. So don't let our present troubles get us down. Give us an audacious confidence! Amen.

SESSION 8

Prayer and All the Fullness (Eph. 3:14-21)

(pp. 147-165)

Summary

Paul slips in and out of prayer throughout Ephesians, giving the whole letter a prayed sense. "Paul lives his prayers," Peterson writes. "He is praying even when he doesn't know he's praying" (p. 148). Growing up *in Christ* means everything about us is *in Christ*. Everything gets prayed. Nothing gets left out.

As Paul prays, the relationship between Jesus and the church comes to the center. As much as we try to separate the two, it's impossible. As Sinatra sang, "You can't have one without the other." And just as Jesus is fully human and divine at the same time, so too is the church. And just as it is both difficult and vital for us to retain Jesus' dual nature in our relationship with him, we need to keep the human and divine nature of the church always in our imagination, neither diluting nor compromising either element. Eleven times in Ephesians, Paul places Christ and church side-by-side as inseparable.

When the divine element of church is reduced or ignored, the human element takes over. Performance, production, hyped-up liturgy, and prayerless theology result. When the human element is bypassed, everything is over-spiritualized. People are reduced to souls to be saved and the saved are run through a series of Bible studies, evangelistic programs, and prayer events. The first loses God but develops impressive religion. The second loses its humanity but develops an impressive spirituality.

33

Vigilance is required to keep the dual nature of both Christ and church united. Failure to do so is disastrous.

Bowing the knee in prayer is both an act of reverence and an act of voluntary defenselessness. There's an offering of self and an inability to run away. The bowed knee posture of prayer sets aside any self-agenda as it waits for God.

There's something about simply being human that draws us to prayer. But we tend to either give up on it or lose its personal nature. Living in a culture that uses language impersonally, we easily adopt this form of speaking in our praying. The world gets objectified. People get thingified. God becomes an impersonal, Star Wars–like force. But because the three-personed God can be known only personally, prayer can only be personal. To regain the personal and all-pervading nature of prayer, we turn to the 150 prayers of the Psalms.

Because Christ and church are so inseparably interwoven, the nature of our relationship with one parallels our relationship with the other. If we are functional with one, we are functional with the other. If we are intimate with one, we are intimate with the other. This also means that we never pray alone, even when we are by ourselves. A Christian in prayer is always in the company of the church.

Generally, we start our prayers for others with intercession, asking God to fill a need, and Paul intercedes in Ephesians with exuberance. But Paul at intercession focuses less on what we don't have and more on what God has in abundance. God is keeping us afloat. We tend to focus on the wind and the waves above, but not on the buoyant water below. God was here before our problems and will be long after. God defines us, not our problems. Sometimes, we need a glimpse into the cupboards of God's abundance to keep us from fearing that we'll starve.

Prayer is both an attentiveness to God and the cultivation of our inner life before God. But it's not our own inner person who's so important. It's Jesus, the Inner Man, who takes up residence in us. What's inside of me is more than just me. God dwells there, too. While prayer does arise from our own inner person, it's easy to become so fascinated by our own spirituality that we divinize it. But Christian prayer is a partnership between our inner person and Jesus, the Inner Man. It moves us out of our self-preoccupation and gets us moving along in a Christ-centered way of life. This non-selfish life is tough for us, but the Inner Man helps us grow into it. But not only is narcissism a problem in prayer; we also

34

tend toward a voyeuristic fascination with techniques and phenomena that pulls us away from relationship with God and others.

There are two common misunderstandings about church. First, that it is what we do. Second, that the "real" church is invisible. The first forgets that the church is actually the work of the Trinity. The second forgets that because God is incarnational, the church is historical. In other words, the flesh and bone, brick and mortar details are important.

Quotes to Consider

"Prayer is the cradle language of the church. This is our mother tongue."
   (p. 147)
"Paul lives his prayers. He is praying even when he doesn't know he's praying." (p. 148)
"The church begins in prayer, stays centered by prayer, and ends up praying." (p. 148)
"When we are dealing with church we are dealing with Christ. When we are dealing with Christ we are dealing with church. We cannot have one without the other — no Christ without church, no church without Christ." (p. 148)
"The unique thing about church is that it is both human and divine."
   (p. 149)
"Church has always been prey to enemy assault and infiltration. It always will be." (p. 153)
"Prayer is the lingua franca of humankind. Everybody prays. At least everybody starts out praying." (p. 154)
"Why is prayer for so many either a personal embarrassment or a political cause?" (p. 155)
"Language at its best initiates and develops personal relationships."
   (p. 155)
"But here's the thing: prayer is personal language or it is nothing. God is personal, emphatically personal: three-personed personal. When we use impersonal language in the most personal of all relations, the language doesn't work." (p. 156)
"A thorough immersion in the Psalms is the primary way that Christians acquire fluency in the personal, intimate, honest, earthy language

of prayer and take our place in the great company of our praying ancestors." (p. 156)

"At prayer we are part of a great congregation whether we see them or not." (p. 157)

"The more intimately we are in relation to Christ, the more aware and relational we are with the body of Christ." (p. 157)

"Our problems don't define us; God defines us." (p. 159)

"Prayer weds what we know of God to a personal responsiveness to God." (p. 160)

"At prayer I am not myself by myself before God: the Inner Man is there, a partner in my praying, speaking the word of God." (pp. 161-62)

"Prayer is not 'getting in touch with your true self,' as is so often said. It is the practice of shifting preoccupation away from yourself toward attentiveness and responsiveness to God." (p. 162)

"It is not uncommon in the Christian way for people to get sidetracked in prayer by becoming more interested in themselves than in God, sometimes to the point of obsession." (p. 162)

"Self-consciousness in matters of prayer is not a good sign, not a sign of health, not a mark of holiness." (p. 162)

"There are plenty of people around — they have always been around — ignorant of or indifferent to both Trinity and Incarnation, determined to remake the church along the lines they have learned from marketers and sociologists. They can be safely ignored. They don't know what they're talking about." (p. 164)

"God does know what he is talking about when it comes to church, even if we do not know what we are talking about." (p. 165)

Questions for Interaction

1. Peterson suggests that Paul prayed even when he didn't know he was praying. What might these non-conscious prayers look like? What about them makes them prayer? How might this understanding of prayer lead to non-praying on one hand or an integrated life of continual praying on the other hand?

2. Like Jesus, Peterson says, the church is both human and divine since it is the body of Christ. The humanity of the church is obvious, but how aware are you of its Spirit-infused divinity? How does the di-

vine nature of the church change the way you think about and relate to it?

3. Do you and your church tend to emphasize the human (performance in worship, activism in mission) or the spiritual (Bible study, prayer, evangelism)? What is good about what you do? What is missing because of an over-emphasis?

4. If prayer is so central to who we are as humans, why do we struggle with it so much?

5. Shaped by our culture's emphasis on the functional and abstract, it's easy for our prayers to become similar. How do you see this in yourself? What would help you be more personal, more relational in your praying?

6. Our poverty is nothing compared with God's abundance. What happens in you when you are more aware of your poverty than God's abundance? What happens to your praying? How might praying help restore a proper perspective?

7. How does Jesus as the Inner Man, living and working in you, change the way you think about yourself? How can knowing he's there and at work in you defuse your self-preoccupation?

Praying from Ephesians 3:14-21 *(The Message)*

Our response to all you have done for us, Father, is to get down on our knees before you — O magnificent Father who parcels out all heaven and earth. We ask you to strengthen us by your Spirit — not a brute strength but a glorious inner strength — that Christ will live in us. We are opening the door and inviting him in. And we ask you that with both feet planted firmly on love, we'll be able to take in with all followers of Jesus the extravagant dimensions of your love. We want to reach out and experience the breadth! Test its length! Plumb the depths! Rise to the heights! We want to live full lives, full in the fullness of you, God.

God, you can do anything — far more than we could ever imagine or guess or request in our wildest dreams! You do it not by pushing us around, but by working within us, your Spirit deeply and gently within us.

Glory to God in the church!
Glory to God in the Messiah, in Jesus!
Glory down all the generations!
Glory through all millennia! Oh, yes!

One and All (Eph. 4:1-16)

(pp. 166-184)

Summary

After three chapters soaking in what God has done and is doing for and in the church through Jesus and the Spirit, Paul turns his attention to our partnership with the Trinity.

We don't need to go anywhere special to meet with God. He's given us a local church. God present to us; we present to God. All of it right there in the middle of our everyday lives. But not everyone chooses church. Many prefer a makeshift, smorgasbord, do-it-yourself belief system tailor-made to fit their lifestyle and temperament. But it ends up a patchy collection of diversions and disconnected happy moments.

But if there is more to God than we can ever hope to understand or experience, the same can be said to be true of his body, the church. Anything we can cobble together on our own will be thin and patchy in comparison. And so will our maturity.

The one thing that gives shape and direction, purpose and guidance to our behavior is God's call. We are called. We have a calling (or vocation), not a job. A job is something you're over and done with once it's completed. A calling is comprehensive, pulling in and giving order to every corner of our lives. We are not just called individuals, but a called community.

There are three basic kinds of speech in church: preaching (kerygmatic speech directed at the will), teaching (didactic speech directed at the mind), and discerning (paracletic speech directed at behavior). Preaching is the most obvious with its dominant role in worship. Because this new life in Jesus requires rethinking our whole lives, teaching comes in second. Discernment, being an informal conversation, has no official time or place and is often not even noticed. It takes what has been preached and taught and works it into the awkward fabric of everyday life, providing comfort and encouragement where needed. Discernment is the often missing and yet vital form of speech essential for maturity, moving us from imperative preaching and informative teaching to personal particulars that enable us to grow into what we know. Paracletic language is Paraclete language, Holy Spirit language. The only workable context for discernment is in a loving community of people who are living discerning lives themselves. If it's not personal, it's not discerning.

The Henry Adams–coined word *deometry* means "taking the measure of God as the unity that produces diversity" (p. 177). The unity of God and of church and of our own lives in Christ each produce diversity. Over time and as we mature, our diverse lives fall into step with God's, finding a single rhythm and direction.

Our culture values speed and consumption, not age or maturity. We spend our time scheming how to do or get what we want instead of learning the maturity of getting along without. To our great frustration, Peterson writes, "There are no maps to the mature life, and certainly not to the mature life in Christ. Growing up involves the assimilation of nothing less than everything . . ." (p. 180). Mapless, we need to give up our attempts to think about what we need, as attractive as one-answer solutions may be.

While church is the context for growing up in Christ, it is not a gathering of the nicest people in town. It is not a gathering of the already mature, but of those who are in process. Most have a long way to go. None are ideal. Neither passion nor celebrity status are marks of maturity. It comes through the commonplace.

No maps. No super-spiritual celebrities. No shortcuts. It's a long, slow process of becoming that slogs through the dark and empty but step-by-step leads us to maturity to the full stature of Christ.

Quotes to Consider

"God created church as a place on earth accessible and congenial for being present to us, listening to us, and speaking to us on our home ground." (p. 167)

40

"Church at its simplest and most obvious is a protected place, an available time for God to have conversation with us and for us to have conversation with God in company with God's people." (p. 167)

"There is far more to God, who he is and what he is doing, than we can cobble together out of our own resources. And there is far more to us, our earthly life and our eternal souls, than can be comprehended by making a mosaic out of shards of beauty." (p. 168)

"God's word to us is inherently a call, an invitation, a welcome into his presence and action." (p. 169)

"The calling gives us a destination, determines what we do, shapes our behavior, forms a coherent life." (p. 169)

"Vocation, calling, is a way of life. A job is different. A job is an assigned piece of work. When the work is done, the job is over and we go back to being just ourselves, free to do anything we choose to do. A vocation, by contrast is comprehensive" (p. 170).

"Preaching is directed to the will, calling us to decide on and follow the way of Jesus." (p. 172)

"The Christian life involves re-understanding our entire lives and the whole world in the light of God's revelation." (p. 172)

"Teaching is directed to the mind, to knowing the mind and ways of God revealed in Scripture and experienced in church." (p. 172)

"Discernment is conversation directed to the insights and decisions, the behaviors and practices, that emerge from hearing the preached good news and learning the truth of the Scriptures as they then get prayed and embodied in my life where I am just now." (pp. 172-73)

"Paracletic language is the language of the Holy Spirit, a language of relationship and intimacy, a way of speaking and listening that gets the words of Jesus inside us so that they *become* us. It is not new information. It is not explanation. It is God's word on our side, within us, working out the details in the circumstances of our lives." (p. 175)

"Becoming mature takes a long time, with many rest stops along the way; it cannot be hurried. Becoming mature is a complex process that defies simplification; there are no shortcuts." (p. 175)

"The underlying and all-encompassing oneness that is church flows from the underlying and all-encompassing oneness that is God." (p. 176)

"The gospel alternative to this cultural welter of one-answer advice and crafty deceit, seduction and empty promises to a better life, is church." (p. 181)

Questions for Interaction

1. Peterson claims that any attempt to craft a Christian maturity apart from church will fail. What objections might you or others have to this claim? What is it about church community that Peterson believes is essential to growing up in Christ?

2. What is the difference between a calling and a job? What does it mean that the Christian life is a calling?

3. How important are preaching and teaching in the life of your church? How important are the personal conversations of discernment in the life of your church?

4. Who are the voices of discernment in your life? For whom are you a voice of discernment?

5. Our culture's lust for speed and consumption also afflict the church. In what ways do churches choose doing things and getting things over maturity? What would your church look like if its priority was to grow up its community in Christ?

6. There are no maps, no one-answer solutions or programs, for growing up in Christ, because it includes absolutely everything. Is this more frustrating or freeing to you? Why? Where does this leave the programs our churches are always trying?

7. Maturing is a slow, life-long process without shortcuts. Why is this? What shortcuts have you tried? Why do we keep falling for shortcuts?

Prayers

Lord we want to walk — no, run! — on the road you called us to travel. No more sitting around on our hands. No strolling off, down some path that goes nowhere. Give us humility and discipline so we can do this not in fits and starts, but steadily, pouring ourselves out for each other in acts of love, alert at noticing differences and quick at mending fences.

As we travel this same road, keep us together, both outwardly and inwardly. In you, we have one Master, one faith, one baptism, one God and Father of all, who rules over all, works through all, and is present in all. Because of you, everything we are and think and do is permeated with oneness.

In your great generosity, Jesus, you have given each of us our own gift. You have filled heaven and earth with your gifts! You have given us gifts of apostles, prophets, evangelists, and pastor-teachers to train us in skilled servant work, working within your body, the church, until we're all moving rhythmically and easily with each other, efficient and graceful in response to you, fully mature adults, fully developed within and without, fully alive like you.

Please, keep us from prolonged infancies. We know you want us to grow up, to know the whole truth and tell it in love — like Christ in everything. Help us take our lead from Christ, who is the source of everything we do. Jesus, keep us in step with each other. Your very breath and blood flow through us, nourishing us so that we will grow up healthy in God, robust in love. Amen.

SESSION 10

Holiness and the Holy Spirit (Eph. 4:17-32)

(pp. 187-202)

Summary

Paul's "therefore" in 4:17 is a major transition, but not an abrupt one. What comes next pours out of what came before. We don't get what comes next without what came before. It's a continuation. The spotlight has moved from God to us, but our part is nothing without God. We are now into the Holy Spirit's work in us to live a God-fashioned life.

Just as rock climbers plan their ascent and put in protection as they climb because of how dangerous their sport is, we need to do the same in the dangerous world of church.

We are always beginners in this Christian life. The problem is that we get practiced at the culture of church and start looking like experts. And seeming competent is something we all like — far worse than the long, hard road of continued maturing. Strangely, this numbing competence is something dabblers are immune to. Dabblers are always beginners. The danger comes when we lose our sense of being beginners and start taking over.

The Greek and Roman imagination was shaped by mythologies with celebrity gods in a way similar to our TV- and movie-fed celebrity culture. Therefore, Peterson says, "Sexual immorality and violence permeated the supernatural in that culture" (p. 193). In both cases, we have a huge spiritual imagination, but impoverished morality. One doesn't translate into the other. What makes the difference is Scripture and the Jesus story which provides an alternate story with an alternate imagination and an alternate way of living. It would have been so easy to embrace this new Jesus gospel while retaining the values and practices of the surrounding culture.

We don't start with morality. We don't get God by moral muscle building. But once we have entered into what God is doing, moral behavior gives shape to the resurrection life. So, once we've heard the Yes of the gospel, we hear a No to our culture's immorality and find ourselves free and clean and whole in an unimagined way. This is like an artist's use of negative space, an emptiness that keeps the clutter out, that leaves space for God.

Leaving space that keeps us from distracting ourselves from what God is doing is important, because God is doing way more than we see or even imagine. And the amazing thing is that God doesn't want us to simply watch him at work, but to get in on it as participants. If we're too busy, we'll both miss seeing what he's doing and miss joining him in it. The Holy Spirit is the person of the Trinity who quietly gets us in on God's work. The Spirit doesn't keep his distance from us, but is very present to us. At the same time, the Spirit isn't flamboyant, making a show out of what he does in us.

The Holy Spirit provides the content and energy for the righteous life God is maturing in us, but he does so personally, relationally. He forces nothing on us. Therefore, it is possible to resist and grieve the Spirit. We walk all over him, and yet he is ever courteous with us.

Quotes to Consider

"Life in the church is dangerous." (p. 190)

"We become so diligent in learning about and working for Jesus that our relationship *with* Jesus erodes. The constant danger — and this has been going on a long time in church — is that we take on a role, a religious role, that gradually obliterates the life of the soul." (p. 190)

"Faith is life at risk. Love is life at risk. Worship is life at risk. Familiarity with God and church and congregation can dull awareness of the stakes involved so that we forget to put in protection." (p. 191)

"Humility recedes as competence increases." (p. 191)

"Jews had centuries of thorough schooling in moral behavior that tilled the soil of the heart for receiving the gifts of God and growing in righteousness and holiness, the two summarizing words that Paul uses to designate life lived appropriately in church in response to God." (p. 194)

"The Christian life doesn't start with moral behavior. We don't become good in order to get God. But having been brought into the operations of God, moral behavior provides forms for maturing in a resurrection life." (p. 194)

"Moral acts are art forms for arranging and giving expression to resurrection." (p. 194)

"The negatives are important as we find our way into the practice of resurrection. They keep the clutter down." (p. 196)

"The negatives don't define our lives. God's positives define us. What the negatives do is leave room for the main action, God's action." (p. 196)

"When we talk too much or do too much, we get in the way of what God is doing. We become a distraction." (p. 197)

"God is active, incredibly active, active beyond our imagination." (p. 197)

"The doctrine of Trinity is the church's way of thinking about God that keeps all of these operations of God together and in relation to one another." (p. 197)

"God can never be understood as an abstraction, as an idea, as a principle, as a truth, as a force." (p. 198)

"We are not spectators to all that God is doing but insiders." (p. 199)

"Holy Spirit is God present with us, making us personal participants in all his work, empowering us to be present in all his work." (p. 199)

"When God brings us into this Holy Spirit life of participation, he doesn't make a show out of it." (p. 199)

"The Holy Spirit is a quiet but powerful nurturing presence." (p. 200)

"What we must realize in all of this is that the Holy Spirit is above all courteous. There is no coercion, no manipulation, no forcing. The Holy Spirit treats us with dignity, respects our freedom." (p. 202)

Questions for Interaction

1. Where have you gotten familiar with church and tried to take over? How can you retain a beginner's sense of wonder and receptivity after years of church life?

2. Why doesn't Paul just transfer his enthusiasm for what God does to an equivalent enthusiasm for what this congregation can now do with and for God? Why doesn't he challenge them to "do great things for God"?

3. Just like the ancient Greek mythologies did then, the stories of TV and movies shape our imaginations now, and often in negative ways. In what ways are we at risk of simply adopting the values and practices of our surrounding culture because of listening to its stories? How does the biblical story shape an alternate way of life? Which story are you most shaped by, the biblical story or the dominant culture's story?

4. "No" is a freedom word, cutting out the clutter and leaving space for God to work. What behaviors has God freed you from (or is he freeing you from) by saying No to them? Why do we resist God's loving No?

5. Some people have no sense of the Holy Spirit's presence or action in their lives and others talk about it in extravagant terms, neither of which are the way the Spirit works. Why are these two extremes so tempting? Which are you drawn to?

6. Whenever we dismiss or reject the Spirit or take over our lives, we grieve the Spirit. Imagine the level of rejection you hand to the Spirit on a daily basis. How is it that the Holy Spirit puts up with this kind of treatment?

Praying from Ephesians 4:17-32

God, please, keep us from going along with the crowd, the empty-headed, mindless crowd. They've refused for so long to deal with you that they've lost touch not only with you but with reality itself. They can't think straight anymore. Feeling no pain, they let themselves go in sexual obsession, addicted to every sort of perversion.

Keep us from that kind of life. We have learned Christ! We are trying to pay careful attention to you, Jesus, having been well instructed in the truth precisely as we have it in you. We're done with the excuse of ignorance. Help us cut out everything connected with that old way of life. It's rotten through and through. Help us get rid of it! And then wrap us up in an entirely new way of life — a God-fashioned life, a life renewed from the inside and working itself into our conduct as you accurately reproduce your character in us.

End our lies, end our pretense. Fill our tongues with the truth.

When we get angry with sin and injustice, help us to not stay angry, to not go to bed angry, to not give the devil that kind of foothold in our lives.

When we're tempted to steal, give us honest jobs so that we can help others who can't work.

Watch over our tongues. Instead of our sometimes foul or dirty talk, give us only what helps, each word a gift.

We don't want to grieve you, God. We don't want to break your heart by the way we live. We want your Holy Spirit, moving and breathing in us, to be the most intimate part of our lives, making us fit for yourself. What a great gift your Spirit is!

Instead of our sometimes cutting, backbiting, profane talk, help us to be gentle with one another, sensitive, forgiving one another as quickly and thoroughly as you in Christ forgave us. Amen.

SESSION 11

Love and Worship (Eph. 5:1-20)

(pp. 203-224)

Summary

There's a huge difference between participation and application. Participation is entering into what God is doing. Not only is application a taking control of what God is doing, but it's completely external to us. We apply bandages to bleeding cuts. We enter into something much bigger than ourselves when we participate.

God's very own life is lived in us by the Spirit. Because of this, God is not so much a truth to be believed in as a life to be lived.

But left to ourselves, we'd get this all wrong. We'd get God wrong. We'd get ourselves wrong. We need Scripture — with all its stories of those who have walked this path before us — and Jesus to keep us safe from the lies of the devil and the culture we find ourselves in.

The world has little time for love and worship. It prefers the practicalities of education, technology, propaganda and advertising, legislation, money, and war. But love and worship are central to our practice of resurrection.

We are defined as the beloved and commanded to love. It is our identity and our practice as those who imitate the God who is love. But this word that is so resolutely personal becomes one that destroys persons, turning them into objects to be used when in the hands of the world. There are two main ways we do this.

First, we eroticize love. Eroticized, love is nothing but copulation, a thrill to be consumed. But by reducing love to sex, we lose our ability to truly love. Both we and the word are ruined. Sex is good, Peterson writes, "but love reduced to sex, depersonalized for mere consumption, whatever the initial pleasures experienced, soon turns ugly, degrades and eventually destroys intimacies" (p. 211).

To help restore biblical love during an equally eroticized era, St. Bernard of Clairvaux wrote of four degrees of love: 1) loving one's self for one's own sake; 2) loving God for one's own sake; 3) loving God for God's sake; and 4) loving one's self for God's sake. When we grow into the fullness of love, we find ourselves loving and fully loved as God always intended: with his love for us being expressed both in our love for him and for ourselves.

Second, we technologize love.

We are most ourselves when we love. But our worst failures come in our attempts to love. We are all incompetent at it and are tempted to give up on it. We'd prefer to do something we're good at, something we get pats on the back for doing. So, when we fail at love, we try to improve our skills, just like we would improve a golf swing. But love isn't a skill, it's a relationship, and it's a relationship that can't be truly entered apart from God, because love originates in God. Reading books, watching videos, taking classes on love (e.g., parenting, marriage, and other classes) don't produce authentic love because they aren't personal.

Church is the best place to learn love. Mixed in with an awkward band of people at various stages of maturity, we actually have the prime conditions for learning love. Why? Because we are all committed to learning love in the context of real relationships with God and community.

Love is learned in the context of worship, where we immerse ourselves in the sacrifice of Jesus, loving him for his sacrifice and joining him in sacrificial living. This only takes place in gathered worship where conditions, as Peterson writes, "do not cater to our personal needs or preferences but honor the priority of God" (p. 217). A God context. A community context. Here we learn love.

In worship, we bring everything that we are together as a community before God, reenacting our salvation through actions like Passover and the Lord's Supper. We lose this relational nature of worship when we turn it into a commodity for consumers out shopping for spirituality.

Even though love and worship are at the core of what church is all about, we are consistently inept at both. But that's because competence is never achievable with either. We never master sin. Therefore, Peterson writes, "if we want to embrace a truly Spirit-formed church, we must embrace the messy conditions . . ." (p. 221). Quit fussing and get used to it.

The not-doing of worship helps us move from the noisy self-importance of immaturity to the quiet contentment of obediently humble maturity. The contrast between wine and the Spirit in Ephesians 5:18 actually continues this theme. Rather than whipping up enthusiasm during worship in a way that mirrors the drunken ecstasy of Dionysius worship, we are to engage in harmonious singing of Spirit-filled worship. Again, we have noisy, emotion-riddled self-preoccupation versus something that may be less thrilling, but is far more relational, both with God and other worshipers.

Quotes to Consider

"'Application' seems to suggest that once we know who God is and what he does, it is up to us to take charge and get it put into action. Nothing could be more misleading. God is as thoroughly involved in our participation as in his Revelation and Incarnation." (pp. 203-4)

"Father, Son, and Holy Spirit are not merely truths to be learned and believed. They are to be lived." (p. 204)

"Watch what God does, and then do it his way. Like children who learn proper behavior from hanging around their parents, be imitators of God, keep company with God." (p. 205)

"Left to ourselves, most of what we imagine God to be and do is wrong. Nearly all of what our culture tells us that God is and does is wrong." (p. 205)

"We require a continuously repeated immersion in the revelation of God in the Scriptures and Jesus as protection against the lies of the devil." (p. 205)

"To love and worship in contemporary America . . . is to be dismissed to a dustbin of irrelevance." (p. 206)

"The eroticization of love empties it of everything except genitals and lust, reduces the person who loves and the person loved to consumers of ecstasy. And as with any life dominated by getting some *thing*, it finally incapacitates him or her from being some *one*. The more a person *gets* the less he or she is." (p. 210)

"God's love permeates our love for God. There is a mutuality in mature love." (p. 213)

"When we love we are most ourselves, living at our very best, mature." (p. 213)

"When we worship we become participants in that offering and sacrifice [of Jesus], and over time that participation permeates our lives with the same love in which Christ loves." (p. 216)

"Worship [in the Hebrew Scriptures] was an act of a people, a congregation, gathering before God offering sacrifices, various sacrifices providing a kind of sign language for all the ways in which they brought their failed or needy or grateful lives to God." (p. 218)

"Worship is fundamental to the practice of love. Love is not a solitary act; it is relational." (p. 219)

"There is not much chance of growing to the measure of the stature of Christ in a place of worship that markets goods and services stamped with a God logo." (p. 219)

"If banks were as inept at handling money as the church is in handling love and worship, they would be out of business within a week." (p. 220)

"Church is not a performing arts center for love and worship." (p. 221)

"There are no flu shots against sin." (p. 221)

"Christian maturity is not a matter of doing more for God; it is God doing more in and through us." (pp. 222-23)

"Immaturity is noisy with anxiety-fueled self-importance. Maturity is quietly content to pursue a life of obedient humility. Christian worship is an intentional act of redressing the proportions. . . ." (p. 223)

Questions for Interaction

1. Unaware of God, the world dismisses love and worship as nice but impractical. Is that something we should be worried about? Is it really all that important to seem relevant?

2. What are the ways our culture reduces love to sex or romance? How does this destroy both love and sex? How might defining oneself by sexual practice be the ultimate in losing love?

3. What are the ways our culture tries to technologize love? How does

a skills-oriented approach to practices we associate with love actually undermine the relational nature of love?

4. Why is the awkward gathering of messy people called the church the best place to learn and practice love? How does the mess lead to love? How does the God-orientation lead to love?

5. What is the relationship between love and worship? How does the sacrificial nature of both deepen them?

6. Why do we always remain inept at both love and worship? How does this incompetence move us from being oriented toward skills and back to relationships?

7. Why do we often opt for individualistic enthusiasm in worship over loving harmony in the Spirit?

Praying from Ephesians 5:1-20 *(The Message)*

God, we're watching what you do. Like children who learn proper behavior from their parents, we're watching so we can do what you do. But mostly what you do is love us. We want to learn a life of love, too. Jesus, we've been watching how you love us: not cautiously, but extravagantly; not trying to get something from us, but giving everything of yourself to us. That's how we want to love, too.

Help keep our love from turning into lust, setting off a downhill slide into sexual promiscuity, filthy practices, or bullying greed. Wean us of gossip. Make thanksgiving our dialect.

Help us stop using people or religion or things just for what we can get out of them.

Keep us from getting taken in by religious smooth talk. We know you get furious with people who are full of religious sales talk but want nothing to do with you.

After groping in the dark, we're out in the open now. Your bright light makes our way plain. Help us figure out the things that will please you — the good, the right, the true — so we can do them. We don't want to waste our lives on useless things. We want to pour our lives into your things. We want to make the most of every chance we get in these desperate times.

Instead of careless, unthinking lives, we want to understand what you, our Master, wants.

What we really want is to drink your Spirit, huge draughts of your Spirit. We want hearts so full that they spill over in worship as we sing praises over everything, taking any excuse for a song to you our Father in the name of our Master, Jesus Christ. Amen.

Household and Workplace (Eph. 5:21–6:9)

(pp. 225-250)

Summary

There is nothing of God or gospel that can't be lived. Nothing is more practical. When we abandon the unglamorous ordinary for the so-called spiritual, we miss out on where the real work is going on, guarantee perpetual adolescence, and cause the ignored ones around us to suffer. It is in the ordinary details of life, not just in worship, that faith is truly lived out.

Named people. Specific places. If it doesn't work here, it doesn't work at all. There's nothing esoteric about practicing resurrection. Home and workplace (or school) are where we spend most of our time and are therefore the primary contexts for living and maturing in Christ.

Interestingly and to our dismay, we are not offered expert advice on how to excel in home and workplace. Paul in Ephesians addresses these primary relationships, but he does so with only a few well-chosen words. Our culture churns out endless volumes on marriage and parenting and business. Paul is focused and brief. Instead of offering Christianized counsel on these topics, Peterson writes of Paul, "What he does is replace our understanding of our already culturally defined roles with a Christ-defined role" (p. 233). Every culture has its way of defining these relationships, but here Christ is redefining them. Everything is done "as to Christ" or "in the Lord" or "under the Master." Same stuff. Completely new orientation.

Part of the reorientation is, again, this move from the abstract to the personal. Our job is not to become the best abstractly loving people we can be, as if love is something that can be achieved by taking an online course. Our job is to love the specific people we deal with on a daily basis in Christ. This requires ditching our winner-loser thinking.

Reverence for Christ is where this all begins. We need a sense of God, of The Holy. When we deal with people, we don't deal with functionaries; we deal with God alive in us. There is "More" here than meets the eye, a sacredness that requires awe. Without this reverence, we reduce people and things into "nothing but" their parts.

Marriage can be the best or worst of all relationships. Peterson writes, "No other relation that we enter into is more complex and difficult and demanding, or fulfilling and pleasurable and satisfying" (p. 238). Both marriage and church refuse to let us get away with individualism, showing it to be the sin of self-idolatry. The visibility of marriage helps us see what church really is, both in the visible human relationships and in the invisible relationship with God. Church exists in the in between, between visible and invisible, between human and divine.

Jewish writer Martin Buber gave determined witness to the centrality of relationship, both in who God is and in who we are as humans. He defined three kinds of human relationships which also shape our relationship with God:

I-It — This is objectification, depersonalization, reducing that other to an It, a function to be used, controlled, or dismissed, not related with.

Us-Them — This is division, fracturing, demonizing into an enemy anyone who disagrees with or stands in the way of us, our programs, our vision, our strategy.

I-You — This is personal, relational, seeking a real encounter with the other for who that person is and thereby enabling me to become more myself in the process.

Too often, we relate to God as an It, as a force to empower us or comfort us. But God as Trinity is entirely relational. When we relate in I-It fashion, we lose our relationship with God, with others, and even with ourselves. We are always in danger of turning church into another set of I-It relations. At the same time, church is God's gift to us to restore us to our basic I-You form of relating.

A relationship is not a something. You can't see or touch it. It is a between — between you and me — a space that enables us to *I-You* each other, just as God *I-Yous* us by his Spirit. Living by the Spirit is an entry into mystery, into something beyond our control, into something we can't contain, into something we can only receive. Although we can treat God like an idea to be discussed, an experience to be savored, and a power to be used, these are all I-It relations, distorted relations. The Spirit is constantly drawing us back into I-You relating with God and each other.

Quotes to Consider

"There is nothing of God that is not livable by us." (pp. 225-26)

"If we thought the world around us was divided into secular and sacred and that it is the Christian's assignment to specialize in the sacred but just put up with the secular, we can think that no longer." (p. 226)

"Great things for God are quite wonderful. Little things for God are in one sense even more wonderful." (p. 227)

"Christian faith is a way of life, not an impregnable fortress made up of ideas; not a philosophy; not a grocery list of beliefs." — Kathleen Norris (p. 227)

"The *practice* of resurrection begins in household and workplace. And we never graduate to higher ground." (p. 230)

"We do not become mature on our own." (p. 232)

"Church refuses to individualize our identity, refuses to put us in charge of our own growing up, but insists that we are 'members of one another' and 'subject to one another.'" (p. 232)

"Every aspect of our family and work life is redefined in relation to Christ rather than to what we have grown up with as wives to husbands, husbands to wives, children to parents, parents to children, slaves to masters, masters to slaves." (p. 233)

"Maturity is not analogous to a body-building regimen in which we lift weights to build our muscles to the max, and then periodically stand before a mirror to examine our progress." (p. 234)

"Maturity does not come about by making the most of ourselves by ourselves; it is making the most of personal relationships." (p. 234)

"Without 'reverence for Christ,' the counsel 'be subject' reduces us to doormats." (p. 235)

"'Fear of the Lord' is the most common phrase from the Hebrew Scriptures for an appropriate life attitude, our learned response for responding adequately to God's word and God's ways." (p. 235)

"A God without holy mystery is not a God to worship on our knees but a cheap idol to be used on demand." (p. 236)

"We may be the proud owners of the most thoroughly irreverent mind-set in human history. Americans as a whole have a minimal sense of The Holy." (p. 236)

"Holy fear has energy in it. It attracts us to something that is beyond us." (p. 236)

"Without a cultivated fear, 'out of reverence for Christ,' we inevitably develop habits of irreverence and are liable to the pandemic 'nothing but' disease." (p. 237)

Marriage is "a primary life setting in which the Holy Spirit brings the love and righteousness, the love and singing, the ways we talk and the ways we forgive into the practice of resurrection." (p. 239)

"Most of what the church is, we don't see: all the operations of the Trinity in the ways of Father, Son, and Holy Spirit." (p. 240)

"We cannot make an object of God; God is not a thing to be named. We cannot turn God into an idea; God is not a concept to be discussed. We cannot use God for making or doing; God is not a power to be harnessed." (p. 242)

"There is no humanity without relationship." (p. 243)

"We try to live with an 'It-God,' a God whom we can talk about all we want to but whom we never listen to as a You or address as You. We try to live by keeping our distance from others, including God." (p. 245)

"Life exists only relationally. Everything is connected. God is God only relationally — Father, Son, and Holy Spirit. God creates only relationally. God exists only relationally. God gives only relationally." (p. 245)

"We cannot see a between; we cannot see a relationship. A relationship is an absence of It so that You can be given and received." (p. 247)

"Spirit is the invisibility that gives life to all that is visibility, the internal that animates all that is external, that without which nothing lives." (p. 248)

Questions for Interaction

1. It is easy to spiritualize faith, to focus on ideas and visions and programs at the expense of real relationships. When has someone ig-

nored or walked over you for the sake of some vision or program? When have you done the same?

2. Why do we trade real, day-to-day relationships for programs and ideas? What is attractive about tidy abstractions that cause us to choose them over messy but real relationships?

3. If marriage, parenting, and workplace relationships are so important, why does Paul write so briefly about them? What is his goal in what he does write?

4. Why is a sense of reverence for Christ and of the sacredness of people so important? Why is it almost completely missing in our culture?

5. Why are marriage and church paired? How does marriage show us what it means to be church?

6. Take a look at your basic, everyday relationships and think about how much you relate as I-It, Us-Them, and I-You. How much of the time do you spend in I-It relating? Why do you fall back into I-It relating?

7. How much of your relationship with God is I-It? What would help you move toward more of an I-You relationship with God?

Praying from Ephesians 5:21

Lord, teach us to worship. Give us a deep and abiding sense of holiness that we might carry around with us always a reverence for you, O Christ. May this reverence for you infiltrate every relationship we have, from the intimacies of home to those we rub shoulders with at work or school or wherever you send us in our daily lives. You make every relationship holy. We want to do the same. In Jesus. Amen.

The Wiles of the Devil and the Armor of God (Eph. 6:10-17)

(pp. 251-271)

Summary

As Paul winds up Ephesians, he is free of anxiety or rhetoric. We inhabit a place of blessing. We just need to stand firm in this blessing and not get distracted.

We need to stand firm in the church, this gift of hospitality. We need to not get distracted by trying to attract religious consumers or by trying to fix problems.

We need to stand firm in the Spirit, this gift of relationship with God and one another. We need to not let sin habits erode our ability to relate, resisting anything that depersonalizes.

In our highly consumerist, quickly bored culture, we are constantly and easily tempted by spiritual novelties, abandoning church and relationship for them. But this only perpetuates our immaturity.

We live in hostile country. Enemies abound, but not ones that look like enemies. Earlier in Ephesians, Paul listed obvious sins, sins that we all recognize as wrong, sins that we have laws and other guides to keep under restraint. We need to resist these, of course, but there are evils which are more insidious because on appearance they seem to be good. We are up against the devil's *wiles;* the devil's *methods.* You can't see a method. The evil isn't in the thing. It's in the way the thing is done, the method. We often miss the evil because we like the good result. The evil is in the means, not the end.

The first tip-off about the devil's methods is that they are abstract.

Whereas God's methods are relational, personal, the devil's are abstract. This is why institutions are breeding grounds for evil. Institutions are adept at focusing on lofty goals and steamrolling people to get there. But because they are effective in achieving their goals, the evil either is unnoticed or tolerated.

When we are in dangerous situations, we tend to panic, fight, or ignore the danger. But there is another way for us: to stand firm in Christ. The six items of the armor of God that enable us to stand firm have little to do with us doing anything. They are gifts, not spiritual skills. We fight not by fighting, but by participating in Christ's work of redemption. Peterson writes, "We *are* the weapons. *Who we are* takes precedence over what we do" (p. 261). The weapons aren't what we do, but who we are in Christ.

We are in a battle that requires our full participation. We aren't passive. But the weapons aren't for killing or overcoming the opposition by force. They are the internalization of the life of the Trinity. Truth, righteousness, peace, faith, salvation, the word of God — these things armor us as we grow up in Christ, as we practice resurrection, as we live in relationship with the Trinity in the company of the church. We don't defeat the devil by taking on his methods, but by taking on the life of the Trinity.

Standing firm often feels like failing, because it gains no ground. The devil's methods seem more effective than God's: propaganda seems more effective than truth, money more than righteousness and salvation, technology more than love, violence more than people and praise and faith. But God's slow and imperceptible-seeming methods bring true and far-reaching victories.

As we stand firm in the company of the church, we mature and grow into a prayerful life. Church and Scripture are our teachers in prayer, not increased effort. When we keep company with the saints of church and Scripture, Peterson writes, "we are praying and learning to pray even when we aren't aware of it" (p. 267). Our praying starts with and for the community of church and home where our primary relationships are and moves out from there. By keeping it relational, asking for prayer as much as receiving it, we protect it from falling into cliché.

Concluding Ephesians and other letters with personal names, again, points to the personal nature of all that Paul wrote. These aren't just ideas. This is about something lived in the real world and among real relationships. We grow up in conversation with the Trinity and with one another in church.

Quotes to Consider

"Nothing is ever accomplished in a stampede. . . . Undisciplined energy is useless, or worse than useless. When the tactics of fear are used in Christian communities to motivate a life of trust in God and love of neighbor, habits of maturity never have a chance to develop." (p. 252)

"When religion as novelty spreads, maturity thins out. . . . following Jesus is not a consumer activity. Prayer is not a technique that can be learned as a skill; it can only be entered as a person-in-relation." (p. 255)

"People who hate God express their enmity against God's people." (p. 256)

"There is far more that is wrong with the world than the sum total of what we name as sin and sins. . . . There is evil that rarely looks like evil." (p. 257)

"Most of the people, sometimes all, involved in these institutions have no idea of the accumulation and dispersion of evil going on in their workplace." (p. 259)

"The basic good of money is idolized into the god Mammon; the basic good of language is debased into the lies of propaganda; the basic good of technology is depersonalized into a world of non-relationship." (p. 259)

"The practice of resurrection is thoroughly pacifist, but never passive." (p. 263)

"As we grow into maturity, prayer is the language that increasingly underlies and suffuses all of our language." (p. 266)

"Not all prayers are conscious. Not all prayers can be identified as prayers. . . . Most of us pray a good deal more than we are aware that we are praying." (p. 266)

"It's not that prayer does not involve attentiveness and alertness to God; it's only that it doesn't require a learned skill. Trying harder doesn't help." (p. 266)

"Prayer and 'supplication for all the saints' (Eph. 6:18) keeps prayer from fuzzy generalities and excessive preoccupation with oneself." (p. 267)

"It is always easier to pray for people we don't know and don't have to deal with than for those in our own congregation and home." (p. 267)

"Many of us would much prefer to be in a position to only help others, to pray for them instead of asking them to pray for us." (p. 268)
"Of all forms of language, prayer is most vulnerable to cliché. . . . A cliché prayer is no prayer." (p. 268)

Questions for Interaction

1. In the face of hostility, Paul is free of anxiety or rhetoric. What gives Paul this unhurried, unharried sense? Why do we so easily get distracted from what God has done and is doing right now?
2. There are enemies in this life of following Jesus. Not everyone or everything is on our side. How comfortable or uncomfortable are you with knowing there are enemies?
3. It's not the devil so much as the devil's methods that Paul warns us against. What are the devil's methods? How might they be more dangerous to us than the devil himself?
4. The six items of the armor of God aren't actually weapons or skills, but the life of the Trinity lived in us. What is the difference between skills that we control and use and the life of the Trinity manifest through us?
5. Standing firm often feels like failing, because it gains no ground. When are you most tempted to use the devil's methods (e.g., propaganda instead of truth, technology instead of love) instead of God's methods?
6. How does prayer get reduced from relationship to cliché?

Praying from Ephesians 6:10-24 *(The Message)*

Strong God, keep us strong. Help us to stand up to everything thrown our way in this life-or-death fight to the finish against the devil and all his angels.

Lord, you know that we're up against far more than we can handle on our own. We need all the help we can get, every weapon you have issued, so that when it's all over but the shouting we'll still be on our feet. Truth, righteousness, peace, faith, and salvation are more than words. Work them into the substance of our lives. Your Word is an indispensable weapon. Prayer, too. Keep us praying hard and long. Praying for our brothers and sisters. Praying with our eyes open. Lord, we don't want anyone to fall behind or drop out.

God the Father and our Master, Jesus Christ, you have mixed love with faith and poured it out on us. We live in a world of pure grace and nothing but grace because of you, our Master, Jesus Christ. We love you. Amen.